KITTENS

JEN BESEL

BLACK RABBIT BOOKS

Bolt Jr. is published by Black Rabbit Books
P.O. Box 3263, Mankato, Minnesota, 56002.
www.blackrabbitbooks.com

Michael Sellner, designer; Omay Ayres, photo researcher

Names: Besel, Jennifer M., author.
Title: Kittens / by Jen Besel.
Description: Mankato, Minnesota : Black Rabbit Books, [2020] | Series: Bolt Jr. baby animals | Includes bibliographical references and index. | Audience: Age 6-8. | Audience: K to Grade 3.
Identifiers: LCCN 2019000989 (print) | LCCN 2019002719 (ebook) | ISBN 9781623101459 (ebook) | ISBN 9781623101398 (library binding) | ISBN 9781644660959 (paperback)
Subjects: LCSH: Kittens—Juvenile literature.
Classification: LCC SF445.7 (ebook) | LCC SF445.7 .B47 2020 (print) | DDC 636.8/07—dc23
LC record available at https://lccn.loc.gov/2019000989

Printed in the United States. 5/19

Image Credits

iStock, jaqy: 16–17; Shutterstock: ADA APA DENGAN DESIGN, 14 (cat); Aleksei Verhovski, 18–19; CNuisin, 3, 24; DavidTB, 22–23; ingret, 13; Katho Menden, 5 (cat), 20–21; Keekz Design, 7 (coins); Leonid and Anna Dedukh, 6–7; makalex69, 4; MaraZe, 10, 11; NataVilman, 12; Olhastock, 1; schankz, Cover; SunRay BRI Cattery RU, 8–9; tobkatrina, 21 (inset); Vitalina Rybakova, 5 (butterfly)

Contents

Chapter 1
A Hungry Baby 4
Chapter 2
Food and Homes 10
Chapter 3
Growing Up 16
More Information 22

CHAPTER 1

A Hungry Baby

A little kitten **wobbles** away from its mother. It sees a bug. The kitten jumps to get it. It misses. But that's OK. There are other things to chase. But soon the kitten needs its mother. It's hungry!

wobble: to move from side to side in a shaky way

WEIGHT COMPARISON

newborn kitten

about 3.5 ounces
(99 grams)

Growing Fast

Newborn kittens can't see or hear. They lie near their mothers to stay warm. But kittens grow fast. After a few days, their eyes and ears open. They can see and hear their world.

17 U.S. quarters
about 3.4 ounces
(96 grams)

PARTS OF A Kitten

ears
eyes
mouth

CHAPTER 2

Food and Homes

Kittens are playful and **curious**. Playing makes them hungry. At first, they drink their mothers' milk. But as they grow, their teeth come in. Then they can eat soft foods.

curious: excited to learn

FACT

All kittens have blue eyes at first.

A Warm Home

Pet kittens need warm, safe homes. They need **litter boxes**. They also need beds and food bowls. Kittens like toys too.

litter box: a container used as a toilet for some animals

Top 5 Countries with the Most Pet Cats

France
Russia
China

CHAPTER 3

Growing Up

Kittens have a lot to learn. They learn to clean themselves. They also learn to use their eyes, ears, and noses to look out for danger.

FACT

Cats feel things with their whiskers.

Leaving Mom

At about three months old, kittens can care for themselves. They can leave their mothers.

Most cats are fully grown by their first birthdays. They can soon have kittens of their own.

25

Adult Cat's Weight

up to about 25 pounds (11 kilograms)

Bonus Facts

Cats purr when they're happy.

Kittens have 26 teeth.

There are up to 71 different kinds of cats.

Cats **hiss** when they are scared.

hiss: a sound like a long "s"

READ MORE/WEBSITES

Lynch, Annabelle. *Cats and Kittens*. Animals and Their Babies. Mankato, MN: Smart Apple Media, 2017.

O'Connor, Jane. *Fancy Nancy: Oodles of Kittens*. New York: Harper, an imprint of HarperCollins Publishers, 2018.

Schuh, Mari. *Cats*. Pets. Mankato, MN: Amicus, 2019.

Fun Cat Facts for Kids
www.sciencekids.co.nz/sciencefacts/animals/cat.html

Fun Facts on Cats and Kittens
www.fun-facts.org.uk/animals/cats-and-kittens.htm

Kitten Facts for Kids!
www.youtube.com/watch?v=4bpeGl4p3Ow

GLOSSARY

curious (CUWR-ee-us)—excited to learn

hiss (HISS)—a sound like a long "s"

litter box (LIH-tur BOX)—a container used as a toilet for some animals

wobble (WAH-buhl)—to move from side to side in a shaky way

INDEX

B

body parts, 7, 8–9, 10, 11, 16, 20

F

food, 10, 13

H

homes, 13

P

playing, 4, 10, 13

S

sizes, 6, 19

sounds, 20, 21